Simultaneous Submissions

LB Sedlacek

Acknowledgments

"Family Honor" was originally published in *Alien Budda Zine* – 2020

"Foment the Injury" was originally published in *Alien Budda Zine* – 2020

"Giants in the Sky" was originally published in *Alien Budda Zine* – 2020

"Sanguine Verbiage" was originally published in *Alien Budda Zine* – 2020

"The Flyblown Waggish Whipsaw Charlatan Itinerant Neophyte Gadfly" was originally published in *Poetry Super Highway's Poet of the Week* – Jan 2020

"Your Unwritten Lexicography" was originally published in *Alien Budda Zine* – 2020

"Word Power" was originally published in *Poetry Super Highway's Poet of the Week* – Jan 2020

Also by LB Sedlacek

Alexandra's Wreck - Kitty Litter Press

Four Thieves of Vinegar & Other Short Stories - Alien Budda Press

The Adventures of Stick People on Cars - Alien Buddha Press

The Architect of French Fries - Presa Press

The Poet Next Door - Cyberwit

Words and Bones - Finishing Line Press

Contents

Section One

Interlude

Section Two

Section One

In Memory Of

Places we always went together
I look for you
places we stopped and I
remember what we bought
restaurants where we always
ate together and we
both always ordered the
same things each time
even though you're gone
and have been for awhile
I still search for you
at every convenience store
in the corner of every booth
and listen for your words
you'd say to the same
people we used to go see
together it's a feeling that
never goes away I still
search for you even though
my mind knows you are gone
my heart still won't let me
believe it.

Giants in the Sky

Two dueling clouds
in the sky
black and dark
a smoky gray
think that they're
going to fight
or maybe die
they are reminders
of parks we've
never been to
plants we've never
grown all seeing
all overbearing encompassing
clouds
you fill us
with awe and
wonder or trepidation
your smoke your
plume rising up
like a nuclear
mushroom smothering cloud
is this our
warning our last
call from the
clouds?

Word Power

Writing by candlelight
with paper and pen
no ink no feathers
no rolltop wooden desk
I write like Benjamin
Franklin or Thomas Jefferson
in the glowing shadows
candles casting off the
perfect snow it glares
and reflects through the
windows a story waiting
to be heard to
be told how we
trekked through the woods
to forage to make
snow cream to toss
icy snowballs or to
sled how we built
a snowman eight feet
high how we built
an igloo or something
like it our hands
wet and cold from
the ice the powder
a snowstorm without power
is something to write
about using pen and
paper and a few
spare words.

Word Power, Take 2

Putting paper to pen
something to write about
using few spare words

a snowstorm without power
the ice, the powder
our hands wet and

cold from building an
igloo or making snow
angels, and a snowman
nearly eight feet tall
we tossed icy snowballs
went sledding and trekked
through woods foraging planning
to make snow cream

I write like Benjamin
Franklin or Thomas Jefferson
in the glowing shadows
candles casting off the
perfect snow it glares
and reflects through the
windows a story waiting
to be heard, told

with pen and paper
no ink, no feathers
no rolltop wooden desk
writing by candlelight using

a few spare words.

Sanguine Verbiage

To chatter
to trill
unnecessary words
wordiness
superfluous words
necessary true
redundant
wording
on the
bright side
blood, phlegm
yellow bile
black bile
bloody blood
take your
cheerful disposition
and shove
it up
your diction
two
words
so unsimilar
how can
this poem
have been
written by
the
same
person!

The Unique Story of the Little Dump Truck

He looks up
and sees a
plane and calls
it a flying
dump truck he
sees a train
he says that
car's moving fast
at summer camp
he jumps on
the pool table
and shouts this
is how you
play pool and
he hits the
cue ball like
he's playing golf
he comes to
breakfast at noon
and asks what's
wrong with his lunch
he's just a
little off in his
own little world
that's what makes
him who he is.

The Flyblown Waggish Whipsaw Charlatan Itinerant Neophyte Gadfly

You new convert you
novice, tyro, beginner
traveling from place to
place especially covering
a circuit performing acrobats
dancers, trainers, dogs
desperately touring the country
or pretending to
have some medical skills
you fake fraud
or bites like flies
annoying persistent criticism
beset with two
or more or more
adverse unpleasant unthinkable
conditions doubly cut
double double the hurt
tainted not bright
not new but seedy
infested with eggs
you exploit for humor
a gallows bird
or maybe sorta human
prank, joke, mischief
practical prankster or not
still all of
this simply suggests the
actual presence of
flies.

Your Unwritten Lexicography

LeLexis
word
speech
a 4th descendant
pretentious
effect
lexiphanic
lex
legal
law
you seem to
use
your
own
lexicon
to make up
your
excuses
stories
none of them
trendy
all
of
them, though, controversial.

Family Honor

Gary Cooper
made films
like you
make beautiful
gestures all
meaningless just
the same.

Deep Rotation

Look out the window through
the woods lights
twinkling making me
envious of the
neighbor's power as we
have none
and later after a
poetry reading sharing
laughs and snacks
over stories of night
terrors and teaching
no one envious of another
poet's tale of a lost child
sleepwalking to the street
safe now (all the same)
we swallow glitter covered
warnings
of being swindled
of being prepared
of being toppled
tweak the heart
all full of hope
now drowned in cement
the only way it
can feel
without
power

and
with loss

still
we go on.

Alterations

Earthen side
overgrown
rounded knoll
hill
mossy foliage
ridge
of ice
language
spoken by
original
inhabitants
in secret.

Foment the Injury

A major fire tonight
near the movie theatre
the message comes in
could be the trucks
could be the frames
whatever it involves furniture
lit up the sky
fire truck sending big
streams of water on
the roof the highway
shut down it looks
like something in the
movies a huge pillar
of thick black smoke
filling the sky like
the fire last year
in the warehouse where
was the night watchman
what was the cause
these abandoned warehouses closed
for lack of sales
too big to be
used for much else
they have many doors
and rooms and places
to get warm in
the cold this night
like last night another
winter storm snow, ice

and barrels and wood
scraps enough to make
a fire to warm
the heart like Janis
Joplin did giving hers
away we sit in
the fog watching snow
skiers and snowboarders twist
and turn down the
slopes the curves the
runs unaware of billowing
black smoke or starving
cold factory warehouse vagrants
sparking up the space
trying to stay alive
trying to stay warm.

Teacher vs Student

We pretend
servile flattery
by heating and then cooling
steel or glass
brittle
less
brittle
at the end of the day
it cools down really slowly
toughening
steel or glass
embracing
our subordinate position
fawning
sycophantic compliance
everything
old
is
new
again
the oldest of human technologies
we may have lost the
battle
but we will set your
DNA
on fire
with
double-stranded
nucleic acid.

The Bookmark Thief

You took my bookmark
I know it was
you how oh how
because it's my bookmark
for my book with
my name and website
right on the front
oh you didn't notice
oh you want to
buy one or two
of course and now
my bookmark is yours!

The Something Else
(In Memory of "insert name here")

24 minutes
off the ventilator
and that was it
there may be a
separate God for children
but this is not it
she fought, they said
it wasn't the chemo, they said
it was something else
something
else
isn't it always something else
and she isn't the first
to lose the battle
can you not think of
someone you know
who isn't fighting
the fight
this fight
where does it come from
how does it happen
why can't we stop it
brains, livers, lungs
breasts, bone marrow
skin
should not have to
battle
this

battle
this bodily war
of which
no species
seems to
be immune
and while we rage war
on each other
physical
territorial
mental
economical
we could join
together
and do
something
it's always
something
we could
fight this
battle
this something else
and
celebrate
our selves
other species
and save ourselves
from
something, the
something
else.

Reply All

Reply
or
All
or
Not
careful
On
the
Buttons
or
Everyone
will
Read
your
Reply

A Book for the Ready

Go with me
carry me in
your deep pockets
carry me as
gold, medication, gems
I am your
one-stop
I am your
ideal
I am your
molding
a Keene bullet
in your pocket

Your Character and the Universe

Fate
universe
control
physical world
preexisting chaos
eternal forms
Plato credits a deity
to create a new
idea
TV show
something
you artisans you
and your
special skills
people work
but someone
behind the scenes
always takes the
glory.

Perfidious Parolles

You are perfidious
so much so
I woke up
in a post-wine
Katzenjammer
unreliable witness
saying whatever suits
your purpose

eventually causing
even cats
or Shakespeare
to wail.

Artemidorus Daldianus

linguistic
dreamer
surge
spin-off
interpretation
soothsayer
dreams
dreamy
just adds to the
oneiric effect

Premonitions of Always Spelling with an X

Your speech
your
language
host and
guest
xenial, xenios, xenos
sensible, sensation, sensitivity
something about
to
happen

Writing Prompts

How could I
have thought it would be
all right?

What's it like to own more
than one pet?

Describe something using only
your favorite colors.

What do you do during the day?
Now tell about what you don't do
during the day (or night) but would
like to do.

(Insert poem or
story
here.)
Now begin.

The Homily Palindrome

assembly
back again
smart wordplay
you drab fool
you aloof bard
magical
tales
all
to carve on
walls

Import/Export

Let's place
an embargo
on your
heart so
you can't
keep trading
it for
another

Interlude

The Donut Shop at Carolina Beach

is right on the Boardwalk and
serves your donuts in a brown
paper bag to go or you can
dangle legs, sit on a stool
at the lime Formica counter
eating the best fried - with a touch
of powdered sugar small - round
donuts you'll ever have. They'll
make you wish you lived close
to the Boardwalk, close to the beach!

The World according to Donuts

I used to know where
every donut shop was
of the donut brand I like
driving miles out of the way
hours out of the way
for those donuts that
taste just like pound cake
buying a dozen at a time.

I used to know
where every donut shop was
of the donut brand I savored
stopping all hours of the night
watching the app on my phone
telling me when the donuts
would be just made
fresh and hot, ready to order.

I used to know where
every donut shop was
of the donut brand I craved
in the grocery stores
driving to more than one store
at a time cutting coupons
stocking up and eating
two or three at a time.

I used to know
where

every donut shop was
but then I bought a
deep fryer so
now I make my own!

Donut Shops across Canada

One year we drove across
Canada from
Niagara Falls to
Detroit and every time
we stopped, we stopped
at a donut shop
because it was the
only restaurant we could find
making us think that
Canadians love donuts
most of all!

Donuts of the Future

will be imaginary
your fingers will stay clean
no teeth to brush
the smell implanted
in the chip in your brain
that's where you'll find
the taste too
your brain will only be
able to imagine the
soft chewy dripping sugary
oily melting goo
but you'll be able to
pick any picture:
(sugar, sour cream, Bavarian,
pumpkin spice, blueberry
chocolate iced, frosted)
of any donut you like.

The future has no calories!

Last Donut on the Mountain (Donuts for Deer)

We always buy a bag of sugared powdered
donuts in one of those crisp clasp closed
triangle bags that puffs the rich smell
of fresh made donuts in your face when
you first open it up the powder poofs
up your nose your fingers lingering
on the tongue the lips the best thing
about waking up high up on the mountain.
It's a treat of a breakfast as we
gaze at the blue green tree tops
the sky, the white puff of clouds.

Section Two

Flibbertigibbet

Shakespeare saw
the   evil
in gossip
     from
     King Lear
but
Sir Walter Scott's
impish urchin
made it stick

meaningless
dickering
over
chatter

Side by Side

Your alibi
insurmountable
finding a
place
to keep
you
hidden the
hurdles
of options
correspondence
and that
one
drunken proposal.

Office Work

this isn't an office
it's a home
this isn't a home
it's an office
notepad
scratchpad
notebook
laptop
smartphone
welcome to your future
the big idea
big ideas
blue jeans
pencils
pens
inactive ideas once a
week
a day or nobody
how many ideas can
you put down in
a day
hire yourself out as
a freelancer
article writer
critic
editor
publisher or reviewer or
writer
did you know there are

56 million wannabe
writers
and you are simply one
of them (yes I made
that number up, but it
reads good, right?)
stapler
sticky notes
tape

I.D.

How can you
truly prove you
are you except
for that piece
of plastic you
carry in your
wallet but it
does you no
good when someone
bumps you and
takes it and
your wacko $2
bills you carry
inside because they
are you and
different like you
and while they
were stealing your
wallet and perhaps
your identity they
took your library
card no problem
cause no one
but writers mostly
read anymore so
what will they
do did they
do the gang
of thugs on

a Charleston block
they call it
New York of
the south for
a reason pickpockets
come here the
weather is better
walk and work
all year long
the tourists creep
creep along the
slick slate sidewalks
even worse from
the rain the
humidity from the
swamps and they
have stolen your
plastic card your
face your #
someone wanted to
give you to
identify you with
wonder what's wrong
with using your
name and losing
the fake plastic
card and the
assigned number oh
maybe there's some
truth to the
horror of being
known not as
a someone but

only as part
of an equation
oh how we
would add up
all the parts
then one by
one two by
two.

Typography of the Heart

You collect hearts
the
way
I collect books
binding, paper, ink
or
fleeting physical qualities
collectible first editions
with
better
content

Copper, Whiskey and Writing

shameful
a writer
who doesn't write
only edits, types
critiques
and maybe
conspicuously bad
or tearing up
and burning work
a sort of still
kin to cognac
now that's a
spouted cup to
get behind

Speech

using words incorrectly
speaking
incorrectly
an ungrammatical combination
of
words
social blunders
sloppy syntax
all good
reasons
to
let you go

Whips and Scorns of Time

Hanging outside on the deck
waiting
for the open mic
      a band
      a Dad and his kids
      a bluegrass singer
a rock band
but where
      where's
where is the poetry
no poets
no lyricists
no poems
where oh where
did they remove
poetry from activity
repressing poets
      quash plans
      to hear impromptu
words and verse
discharge your pens
terminate your keyboards
William Shakespeare is
holding all your
      metaphors
      hostage
how bare the
world the stage

at this open mic
will be without the
          poets
but yet none are
          here
or if they are
          they
are sitting on their
          books
quietly waiting for the
          music
          to
          end.

Would That It Were

I'd be
publisher
artist
writer
entertainer
a collector of
anecdotes

Spectate Me!

Dead leaves and wind
roll out pithy phrases
aimed at that dwarf
of folklore oh garden

statue you're quite clever
holding your own against
wet wind ice cold
snow blazing hot dust cloud
four season four weathers

the young artists draw
attention to their bright
colored attire which critics
argue as pretentious rubbish

oh the composition heats
up and utterances abound

Devolves Into Art

Any
object
could
be
a
work
of
art
natural
formed
objects
the
result
of
natural
forces
or
man-made
artifacts
not
originally
created
as
art
but
displayed
as
such

Landlords

Detoxifying willow leaves
in the belly
is what it's
like to talk
to you via
text, voice, person
all crunchy parts
turned into vapor
and nothing much

offering sustaining substance

kings and queens
would never act
so
easily.

Dire Effects

You false
fake autograph
in books
for sale
illegible anyone
could take
a pen
a quill
and ink
and be
Henry VII
oh the
spurious stock
you of
improper origin

getting out

I work
long hours
I have a pet
the color of
brown, white, black
he's like having
more than one
I try to do
what I can for
the kids
the school
but it's been
a long time
due I'll be
leaving soon
so I brought
in help
thinking it
would be ok
to train them
to take over
for me
to leave it
in better shape
but yet it's
been an
electronic war
gossip on the side
so many things
I never knew

about myself
I've learned
I'm a
control freak
that doesn't
like change
and when
I tell this
to my husband
he laughs and says
they sure don't
know you very
well so now
I've given up
it is what it is
they may be
bankrupt next year
this volunteer parents
group but
even though I care
I cared
I cannot care now
the problem no longer
mine
I've taken the elevator
up and down
and checked out
and some would
say
she's left the
building
we will miss her
others might say

don't let the
door hit you
wait a minute
yeah let
it hit
you on
the way
out!

North Dakota

The hymn of
punching
a song of
hype
folk tales to
fill
in the gaps
plausible
but ultimately unproven
fevers
chop, sock, knockout
fans
come and go
your
story just begun
amongst
blue purple hills
of
histories or mysteries
things
were solved tough
prairie
plains fill with
sockdolager

Stale Origin

A 330 year
old word lost
a younger word
ruinous or decayed
as your brittle
bones your fragile
brains your fortune
decaying as an
old forgotten book.

Frivolous

An impatient audience
is better than
none at all
whistle
hiss
Boo!

Hunting Decoys with Hemmingway

The Roman poet
Martial
was a master
of
the art form
epigrams
you explore the
art
of other ways
their
art you'll never
buy
spare me your
sentiment
things you say
while
you're asking me
why
almost as effective
as
faking on the
ice
or some other
sport
the use of
moves
or actions art
sport
can be wittily

ineffectual
or lead you
to
awakening your art
or
making the goal

Celebration

celebrities and personalities
always
have to have
their
emails, lives hacked
eating
peas off forks
somehow
the real thing
musical
that classical ring
lawyers
would beg to
write
it all out
differently

Be Like Twain

Mark Twain
said it took
him maybe a
week to make
it up all
common you writer
block lack of
decision
indecision
without will it's
impossible to choose
let's go get
some ice cream
or eat a
salad
let's play pool
let's play games
and not swim
it's thundering outside
probably a good
decision
you deficit you
your
loss of will
is
irritating

Follow Lighted Sign Messages

Standard space available
except
when your face
smashes
into the piano
bench
how could you
smell
the upright's keep
wild
sounds descending from
lips
words branched out
swelling
face turned blue
ringing
noises simply uncultivated
almost
like losing your
way
back to camp
fragrances
purged
time cards punched.

Opinions

Permission for peace
means
pacing the room
and
never talking to
you
again.

Theories of You

You fig
you taxes
you farmers
you fink
you gesturer
you slanderer
you flatterer

you chameleon

The Secret of Rain

Unlike the doctor's office
with the soothing aquarium
of dark blue waters
fish of many colors
each drop is a mirror
into your day not
simply mud or wet
how wet the rain
is something often said
how magnifying the drops
a tiny picture in
each one how easily
the moisture moves the
clouds shifting the usual
blues into white and
purple and light pink
a delicate shift of
worlds and words how
lucky to actually see
it how the world
moves with or without
water

Words for Hire

Picking out a card
written in someone else's words
seems ironic
implausible
the poet can't think
of
anything to say so buy a
card
with the words built in
shiny green
on green
green lime
envelope
the world of words
in
green
until it's time to send
the card
mail
(snail mail)
and it's discovered one
word
one simple itty bitty word
would be
maybe
not bring a smile
so that's what
you get
you

poet
you
for hiring some kind
of ghost writing
greeting card writer
to
write
for
you
the words you
couldn't think of
yourself
when you want to
tell someone to
get well but
you can't because
they really will
never be
all well
again

Simultaneous Submissions

1. Double life
    double
    0
    7
    double cheese
    double sauce
    how well do you know
    anyone

2. Books as gifts
    read
    all night
    and eat chocolate
    conjuring up
    the blues
    or wardrobes
    and fawns
    magic toffee
    and fairies
    wishes
    for more pages

3. Same form
    same questions
    written in sixteen
    different ways
    how many ways
    can you ask
    the same
    question?

4. are you a citizen
    do you have any
    income
    do you have trouble
    estimating
    how much you make
    send an email
    it's cheaper than
    stamps

5. Pens
    pencils
    purple, pink, black blue, red
    one
    color
    for
    highlighting
    marking out names
    marking pages
    remembering
    something
    anything
    nothing

6. my double life
    my triple threat
    my quadrupled income
    how many jobs do you
    have?

7. Fortune
    cookies

which one to chose
you friend will take
care of you
you will receive a small
package
a very fun way to
eat
a cookie

8. more cookies
cookie pie
sugar
peanut butter
chocolate chip
simply sample
a bite from
each one

9. Put your name on
the list but your
name cannot be drawn
so you sign up
only to withdraw it
all
but
you don't need the
prize anyway especially since
you helped to furnish
the
gifts

10. Does anyone examine
the care taken

to provide an
interesting stamp on
the
SASE
like ever?

11.   White elephant
Dirty Santa
mystery gifts
like flipping
to a page
in a book
to see what

happens
next

12.   I tend to
write poems
using
words I cannot
pronounce
or phrases I cannot say
making it impossible
to read them out loud

13.   when there's only a
thread
of a storyline
it's simple for it
to break
to dissolve
to disappear

14. cleaning up
     paperwork
     returning messages
     don't you want
     one of those
     answering services
     like actor's
     have?

15. Location, location
     the houses
     the homes
     the places
     used for
     movies

     Does anyone
     (usually)
     scope out
     places
     written about
     in books

16. Windows sometimes
     don't work
     and stay closed
     no matter what

17. If you are constantly
     interrupted how can you
     complete
     anything?

18.   Too many unanswered
      questions

19.   continuing education
       for writers
      look around the room
      look at the sky
      simply
      look

20.   void means void
      void your poem
      or story and
      oops …

21.   Six fortunes
      all come
      true

22.   Where are your
      poetry loving friends
      when you need
      them

23.   Flibbertigibbet
      gossip
       chatter
      onomatopoeic
       Shakespeare used it
       so did Sir Walter Scott
       you silly flighty person

24. It's just an adjustment
     15 minutes
     to tweak a word
     here a comma there
     maybe delete a whole
     paragraph or two you
     don't mind do you

25. I scared you,
     didn't I?

26. Poets stand on their
     own
     poems stand on their
     own

     poets
     poems (should)
     stand
     alone

27. Glitter may dress up
     an outfit but it
     won't dress up a
     sentence

28. Breathe or
     breath
     the only difference
     is the
     E

29.   Fortune cookies x5
      5 fortunes to come
      true

30.   Red, yellow, blue, green
      blinking lights

31.   Rejection letters are
      worse
      than rejection emails
      easier to delete
      the
      emails than to
      burn
      the postmarked uninvited
      letter

32.   Reading lights
      curled around neck
      save your eyes
      (save your stamps)
      let the words
      disintegrate into your
      sleep

33.   Christmas lights of
      blue red green orange
      yellow
      shining through the
      trees

34. how many times can
     you ride a roller
     coaster and not throw
     up

     or how many times
     can you send a
     submission and have it
     rejected

35. Terrain park means
     there are jumps
     wooden boxes to
     hurl over, across

36. I can spell Hawaiian
     but I can't spell
     breath (breathe) oh what
     is wrong with me
     wonders the typo police
     aka don't msg someone
     about their typos unless
     you never make one
     yourself when you write

37. Hot chocolate and a
     veggie burger but can
     you really write well
     in a coffee shop
     or are there too
     many frothy foaming distractions

38.   Don't forget
      to run
      spell check!

39.   Classic small
      hot coffee
      I prefer
      hot chocolate

40.   North Carolina
      grown
      popcorn & pickles
      on
      Christmas Eve

41.   Ad copy counts as
      publishing, right?

42.   Bonus points if
      you publish more
      than one poem

43.   The total package should
      include a cover letter
      with a short Bio,
      sample pages or the
      whole manuscript and the
      ever important SASE or
      an included email address
      and oh yes correct
      postage on the outside
      (optional staples or paper clips
      to hold it all

together depending on the
publication or press preference)
then be sure to
record when it was
snail mailed or emailed
so you can keep
track.

44.   If submitting to more than one
publication, be prepared to withdraw

45.   Swimming in a saline
pool is a different
experience than swimming in
one filled with chlorine

Writing longhand with a pen
is a different experience than
using a pencil or computer

still we swim
still we write

46.   Lighthouse
in the ocean
only way to get to it
is by
boat

47.   Sitting by an aircraft
carrier makes you realize
how small and unimportant
(insert your thoughts here)

48.   If you haven't
       heard from us
       in 4 months
       then you may
       Query

49.   (Blank) publication
        prefers online
        submissions

50.   How to get paid
       but you don't write
       only for money, right?

51.   Peel on stamps
       have replaced
       lick on stamps

52.   The phone booth
       is missing the
       phone so how
       can you make
       an unanswered call

       now

53.   Book signings
       Book events
       Open mic!

54.   How long
       how much more difficult
       to write

a book out on a
typewriter
yet that's how real
books
were written
like vinyl records
to cassette to CD's
and back again
instead of a computer
lab
bring
back
the typewriter Lab
or
Typing 101

55. If only everything fit
in a neat manuscript
box

56. Shouldn't it all
be about the
Work

57. How did Jack Kerouac
write on one typewriter
paper roll without tearing
off at least one
sheet

58. Readings sell more
poetry books than
in stores or
online

59. Withdraw
     accept
     reject

60. Publishing
     there's more to it
     than is it good
     it's also will
     it last and
     more importantly
     will it sell

61. *Contest submissions
     are sometimes
     rigged with the
     winner chosen before
     the contest ends
     (*True story, a well-known
     publication emailed me by
     mistake instead of the
     Judge to say she could
     look at the manuscripts
     but the winner was already
     chosen – I asked for
     a refund)

62. Are all poetry contests
     rigged

63. Pennies
     say 10 of them
     for your thoughts

64.　Books on CD
　　audiobooks
　　replaced books
　　on cassette

65.　The movie
　　or the book
　　which is
　　better

66.　Geysers stay frozen
　　in Winter

67.　How can you call yourself
　　a writer
　　and not read any books
　　writer, writing, reader, reading

68.　I cancelled my
　　subscription
　　yesterday

69.　Online
　　offline
　　it's reading all the same

70.　Read your poems out loud
　　how do they sound to
　　you

71.　Some places never
　　respond to your
　　submission

and
some respond so fast
you may wonder
did they really
read it

72. Galleys are hard to
look at because how
many times can you
read your own poems

73. Just because you don't
like (reject) what I
sent you doesn't mean
I didn't read your
publication or your guidelines

74. Does anyone care if I
use pretty artsy stamps on
my
SASE

75. One thing does
indeed
lead
to another
so keep on plugging
away at that dark
keyboard late at
night

76. Book covers and layouts
the Bio is next

sometimes it's hard
to write in the
3rd person

77. Confessions on paper
     are better
     than ones in person

78. No stories
     are stranger
     than those
     that are
     real life

79. Your funds diverted
     your time inverted
     how to not sell
     yourself or your writing
     short

80. Going with the flow is much
     harder when someone else is
     directing all of the traffic

81. The search for Markets is
     endless
     there are so many and
     then
     to decide what to submit
     a
     whole process all on its
     own

sometimes my poems find homes

82. Content is especially nice
     when you like to
     read
     sometimes there aren't enough
     choices to choose from

83. Poetry readings can range
     from the mundane to
     a slam of words
     what kind of reader
     are
     you

84. Sometimes my words
     don't fit in the
     spaces so neat
     and ready and provided

85. My publisher
     a typewriter
     a computer
     a manuscript
     box does
     such a
     glory exist
     as one
     true publisher
     only for
     you.

86.   Announcements on walls
      are sometimes the best
      ways to get attention

87.   How quick
      can you
      write, submit, publish

88.   Pre-publication date
      isn't that what we
      all aspire to

89.   Submit, reject, revise
      submit, reject, revise
      submit, reject, revise
      X however many times
      then finally
       acceptance

90.   Material can be
      gathered
      a poem in
      your grasp

91.   Removable pockets
      can make
      submissions
      easier

92.   sign for delivery
      but still
      unclaimed
      I guess you didn't

want my
poetry book after
all

93. How long should you
workshop your
poem
or
collaborate before
you consider it
finished

94. Emailing or Calling
and asking for
readings well that
is also part
of the work

95. White snow
equals
starting over

96. A brand new journal
pages clean, clear, crisp
crack it open and
take out a new
pen, preferably with purple
ink and start it
all, the words, all
over again because a
writer never stops writing

97.   I like your poem
      but
      change this word here
      or
      rearrange that one there
      yes
      that makes it so
      much
      better
      but possibly now unpublishable
      stay
      true
      to your own craft

98.   First time I had to
      withdraw a submission
      but because I wasn't
      enrolled in the school
      not for any other
      reason that's pretty good
      odds either way it's
      sliced.

99.   Here are the points of
      your poem
      all laid out and how
      you should
      rearrange it
      (thanks for your input, but
      no.)

100. Finished
     but is it really
     complete
     or is there room
     for
     improvement

     write like you mean it